# MULTICULTURAL LEGENDS & TALES

## Using Multicultural Literature to Teach Creative Thinking and Writing

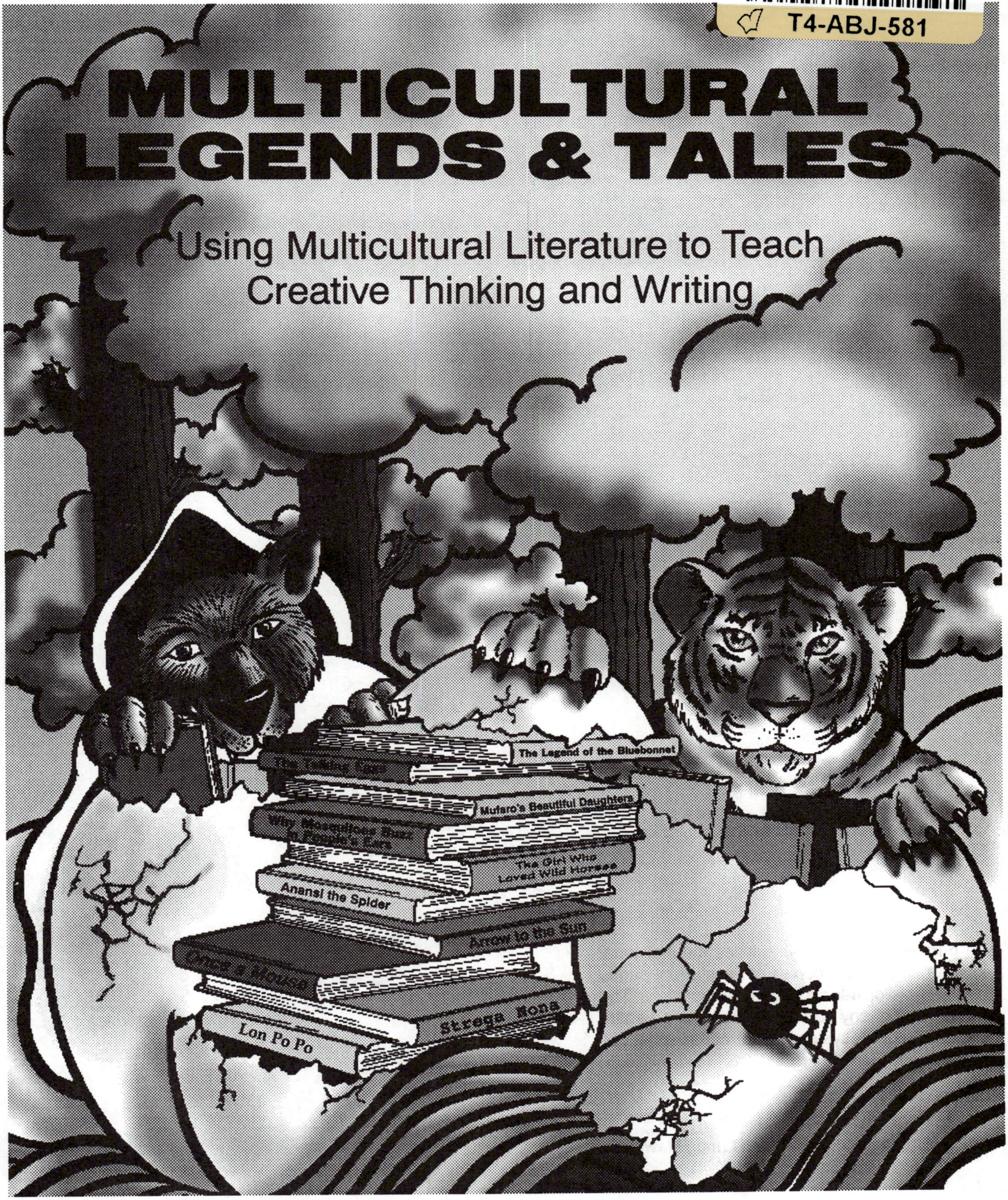

Written by Vowery Dodd Carlile
Illustrated by James Uttel

The purchase of this book entitles the individual teacher to reproduce copies of the student pages for use in his or her classroom exclusively. The reproduction of any part of the work for an entire school or school system or for commercial use is prohibited.

ISBN 1-56644-974-X
© 1995 Educational Impressions, Inc., Hawthorne, NJ

Printed in the U.S.A.

**EDUCATIONAL IMPRESSIONS, INC.**
Hawthorne, N.J. 07507

# Contents

Foreword ................................................................................... v
Introduction ............................................................................... vi

Lon Po Po ................................................................................. 1
Anansi the Spider ...................................................................... 9
Once A Mouse .......................................................................... 19
Mufaro's Beautiful Daughters .................................................. 27
Why Mosquitoes Buzz in People's Ears ................................... 37
Arrow to the Sun ...................................................................... 45
The Legend of the Bluebonnet ................................................. 55
Strega Nona .............................................................................. 63
The Girl Who Loved Wild Horses ............................................ 73
The Talking Eggs ..................................................................... 81

Extra Activities ........................................................................ 91
Crossword Puzzle ..................................................................... 92
Word Scramble ......................................................................... 93
Answers .................................................................................... 94
Pencil Toppers .......................................................................... 95
Bibliography ............................................................................. 96

# FOREWORD

Legends and folk tales have always been an exciting part of my life, both as a young child and as a teacher. I enjoyed listening to them when I was young and teaching them to my students now. I feel we can teach our students a lesson from almost every legend and folk tale. Legends are usually based upon a real person with exaggeration added to the story to make it much more interesting. Folk tales have a moral of the story placed in them to teach a lesson to the reader. Students enjoy legends and folk tales because they see how different situations affect characters' lives. Students sometimes pretend to be one of the characters in a story, experiencing the same adventures as the character. Perhaps through this experience, they will not make the same mistake as the character.

This was an exciting book to write. I was able to read some new stories and reread some that were favorites when I was a child. I hope the students enjoy listening and reading these multicultural legends and tales as much as I have. I would like to thank my husband, Gene, and four children – Coleen, Casie, Corey, and Pat – for their patience and understanding.

**Vowery Dodd Carlile**

# INTRODUCTION

**Multicultural Legends and Tales** includes ten multicultural legends, four of which are Caldecott Medal and Honor Books. Each unit includes activities to promote critical and creative thinking. They include questions based upon Bloom's *Taxonomy of Educational Objectives*,* independent research and planning activities, and creative writing projects. Following the ten units are culminating activities covering all the stories.

Bloom divided cognitive development into six main levels: knowledge, comprehension, application, analysis, synthesis, and evaluation. Most of the questions presented to students fall into the first two categories, knowledge and comprehension. The highest levels are seldom used; they are more difficult to write and, because they have no definite answer, are more difficult to evaluate. Understanding Bloom's Taxonomy will help you provide for your students more and better opportunities to think critically. The following is a brief description of the cognitive levels according to Bloom's Taxonomy.

**Knowledge:** This level involves the **simple recall** of facts stated directly.

**Comprehension:** The student must **understand** what has been read at this level. It will not be stated directly.

**Application:** The student uses knowledge that has been learned and **applies** it to a new situation. He/She must understand that knowledge in order to use it.

**Analysis:** The student **breaks down** learned knowledge into small parts and analyzes it. He/She will pick out unique characteristics and compare them with other ideas.

**Synthesis:** The student can now **create** something new and original from the acquired knowledge. This level involves a great deal of creativity.

**Evaluation:** The student makes a **judgment** and must be able to back up that judgment.

* Benjamin Bloom, *Taxonomy of Educational Objectives*, (New York: David McKay Company, Inc., 1956).

Independent projects can be written to cover any subject using verbs that encourage responses from each of the six categories. These verbs can be used to design independent projects as well as to write your own higher-level questions in any subject area. Verbs for each of the categories include the following:

**Knowledge:** list, know, define, relate, repeat, recall, specify, tell, name

**Comprehension:** recognize, restate, explain, describe, summarize, express, review, discuss, identify, locate, report, retell

**Application:** demonstrate, interview, simulate, dramatize, experiment, show, use, employ, operate, exhibit, apply, calculate, solve, illustrate

**Analysis:** compare, examine, categorize, group, test, inventory, probe, analyze, discover, arrange, scrutinize, organize, contrast, classify, survey

**Synthesis:** plan, develop, invent, predict, propose, produce, arrange, formulate, construct, incorporate, originate, create, prepare, design, set up

**Evaluation:** value, recommend, evaluate, criticize, estimate, decide, conclude, predict, judge, compare, rate, measure, select, infer

These verbs can be used to design independent projects as well as to write your own higher-level questions in any subject area. Below is an example of the chart that I use when creating the independent projects in my books. I have also included a copy for you to reproduce and use when designing your own projects.

| CATEGORY | VERB | TOPIC | PROJECT |
|---|---|---|---|
| *Synthesis* | *Create* | *Strega Nona* | *An original story about how the magic pot might help the world.* |

By incorporating these question-and-project strategies into the curriculum, every child will be given the opportunity to be a creative thinker.

# Independent Projects Chart

| CATEGORY | VERB | TOPIC | PROJECT |
|----------|------|-------|---------|
|          |      |       |         |
|          |      |       |         |
|          |      |       |         |
|          |      |       |         |
|          |      |       |         |
|          |      |       |         |
|          |      |       |         |

# Lon Po Po
A Red-Riding-Hood Story from China

# Lon Po Po

by Ed Young

## STORY SUMMARY

Once, long ago, a woman left her three daughters home alone while she went to visit their grandmother. She warned the children not to open the door and told them that she would return the next day. That evening an old wolf disguised as an old woman came to the children's door. He told the children that he was their Po Po, or grandmother. Shang, the oldest, asked her why her voice was so low. Po Po said that she had caught a cold. The two younger children eagerly let her into the house. So that the children would not see him clearly, the wolf blew out the candle.

When Po Po and the children got into bed to sleep, Shang touched the wolf's tail and said, "Po Po, Po Po, your foot has a bush on it." Paotze felt the wolf's sharp claws and said, "Po Po, your hand has thorns on it." Each time the wolf made an excuse. Shang lit the candle, and the wolf blew it out again, but not before Shang saw his hairy face.

Shang tricked the wolf into going outside for magic nuts. The children offered to climb the tree. Once there, they told him that he must pluck the nuts himself for them to be magic. The children tricked the wolf into tying a rope onto a basket and throwing one end of the rope up into the tree. The wolf got into the basket so that the children could pull him up into the tree. The first time Shang pulled him half way up and let go of the rope. The wolf got into the basket again; this time Shang and Tao pulled him up even higher before letting go of the rope. The children convinced him to try one more time. All three would pull on the rope and would surely get him up into the tree.

The wolf climbed into the basket. The children pulled him to the top of the tree and let go of the rope. The wolf fell to the ground, bumped his head, and broke his heart to pieces. The children climbed down, went into their house, latched the door, and fell asleep. The next day their mother came home with food from their real Po Po.

Like the European tale of Little Red Riding Hood, this tale is based upon an ancient oral tradition. It is believed to be over 1,000 years old.

© 1995 Educational Impressions, Inc.

# Questions & Activities Based Upon Bloom's Taxonomy
## Lon Po Po

**Knowledge:**
1. Why did mother visit Po Po?
2. How was the wolf disguised?
3. Who was Po Po? Guess the meaning of "Lon."

**Comprehension:**
1. How did the wolf explain not meeting the children's mother?
2. Explain how the children tricked the wolf.
3. Did the children follow their mother's directions?

**Application:**
1. Why, do you think, did the mother leave the children alone in their house?
2. Do you have a grandmother? How does your grandmother's voice sound? Try to say something the way she would.
3. Why, do you think, did the wolf blow out the candle as soon as he entered?

**Analysis:**
1. What kind of nut is a gingko? Describe it.
2. Compare this version of Red Riding Hood to other versions that you have read. How are they alike and how are they different?
3. Which character would you like to be? Why?

**Synthesis:**
1. Create another way for the children to trick the wolf.
2. How might the story have been different if Shang had not seen the wolf in the light?
3. Pretend you are the wolf. What other way could you have gotten the children to trust you?

**Evaluation:**
1. What would you do if a stranger came to your door?
2. Could the children have solved their problem without killing the wolf? Explain your answer.
3. Give three reasons why this is or is not a good book to read.

© 1995 Educational Impressions, Inc.

**Pretend to be Lon (the wolf). Convince the children that you are harmless.**

_____
_____
_____
_____
_____
_____
_____
_____
_____
_____
_____
_____

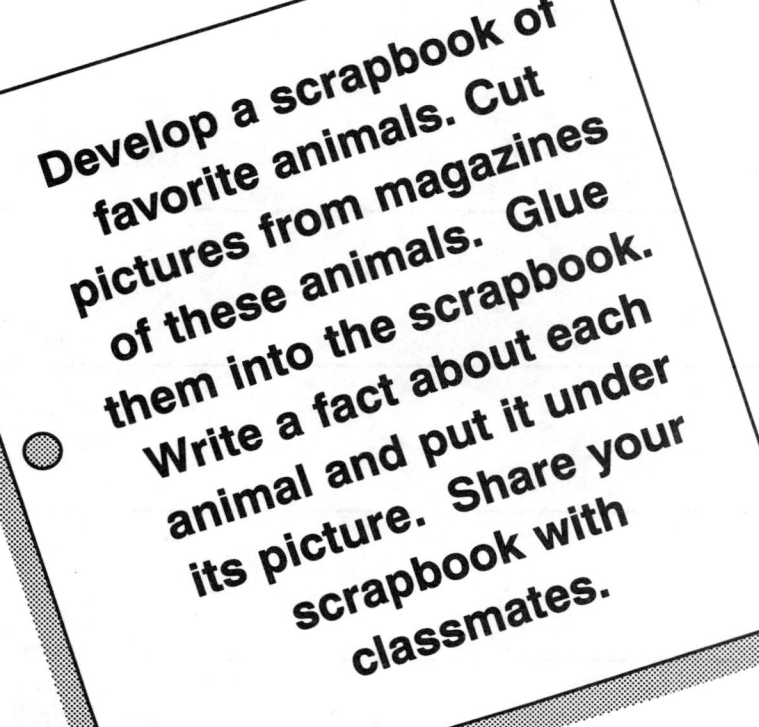

**Develop a scrapbook of favorite animals. Cut pictures from magazines of these animals. Glue them into the scrapbook. Write a fact about each animal and put it under its picture. Share your scrapbook with classmates.**

(paste here)

F<sub>u</sub>N FACTS: _____

_____

_____

© 1995 Educational Impressions, Inc.

**Write an acrostic poem about Lon Po Po.**

L _____
O _____
N _____
P _____
O _____
P _____
O _____

# Create a new version of an old tale.

Lon Po Po is another version of of the Little Red Riding Hood story. Think of a favorite tale. Change it to create another version. For example, you might use the plot in the story of Cinderella and change it into another story.

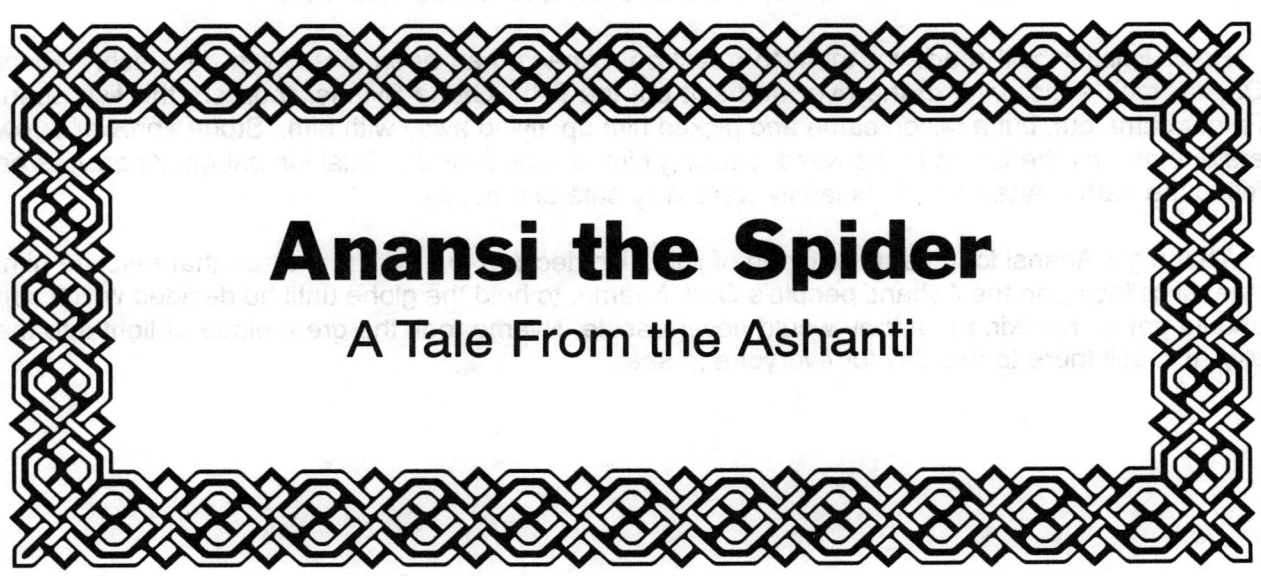

# Anansi the Spider
## A Tale From the Ashanti

# Anansi The Spider

by Gerald McDermott

## STORY SUMMARY

Anansi the Spider had six sons. Each son had a special talent. One son could see trouble coming; the second son was a road builder; the third son was a river drinker; the fourth son was a game skinner; the fifth son was a stone thrower; and the sixth son was a cushion.

One day Anansi took a long trip. He got lost and fell into trouble. The first son saw their father was in trouble. He told the other sons, and they set out to rescue their father.

Road Builder built roads for them to travel on. Anansi had been swallowed by a fish. River Drinker took a big drink of the river and spit out the fish. Game Skinner then cut the fish open. Father came out, but a falcon came and picked him up, flying away with him. Stone Thrower threw a stone and hit the falcon in the head, causing him to drop Anansi. Cushion caught Anansi as he fell to the earth. Anansi and his family were very safe and happy.

That night Anansi found a great globe of light. He decided to give it to the son that rescued him. Anansi called upon the Ashanti people's God, Nyame, to hold the globe until he decided which son should get it. Knowing that they would never decide, Nyame took the great globe of light into the sky. It is still there to this day for everyone to see.

© 1995 Educational Impressions, Inc.

# Questions & Activities Based Upon Bloom's Taxonomy
*Anansi the Spider*

**Knowledge:**
1. Who is Anansi?
2. How many sons did Anansi have?
3. Name three of the sons.

**Comprehension:**
1. Tell about some of Anansi's problems.
2. How did his sons help?
3. Who is Nyame?

**Application:**
1. How might you have reacted had you been Anansi?
2. Explain how you feel about spiders?
3. What is the beautiful white light? How do you know?

**Analysis:**
1. Compare the six sons. Which do you like the best and why?
2. Tell about the art style used by Gerald McDermott. Do you think his style fit the story?
3. Why, do you think, does this legend use a spider as its main character?

**Synthesis:**
1. Create some other problems Anansi might encounter. Write a story plot.
2. What might have happened had the God of All Things chosen one son to receive the prize?
3. Create a way to explain how rain came to be.

**Evaluation:**
1. Read two myths based upon Anansi. Which legend is your favorite and why?
2. How do you feel about Anansi? Explain your answer.
3. Which son do you think helped his father most? Why do you think this?

© 1995 Educational Impressions, Inc.

**S** pinning webs,

**P**

**I**

**D**

**E**

**R**

**Find out more about spiders and report to the class.**

## FACT FILE

SUBJECT: _____

RESOURCE: _____

FACTS: _____
_____
_____
_____
_____

© 1995 Educational Impressions, Inc.

**Get up in front of the class and retell the story. Use hand motions to show what the spiders did to help their father.**

**Choose one of the spiders. Write about how he helped save his father.**

**Anansi the Spider is a legend of the Ashanti people of Ghana. Locate Ghana on a map of Africa.**

**Draw an outline of Ghana on this map. Label Ghana.**

© 1995 Educational Impressions, Inc.

# Write a legend of your own explaining something about nature.

**Examples:** What makes the moon full?
What causes the wind to blow?

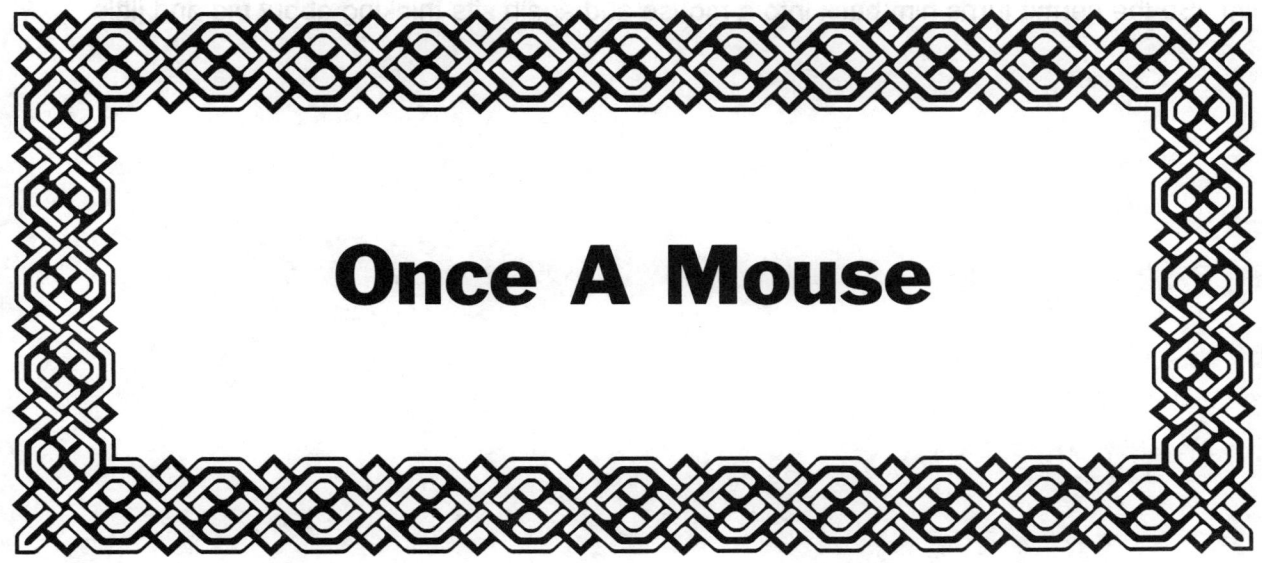

# Once A Mouse

by Marcia Brown

## STORY SUMMARY

This is a tale from ancient India. It tells of an old hermit with magical powers. One day as he is thinking about big and little, he sees a mouse about to be attacked by a crow. He saves the mouse and takes him home. When a cat threatens the mouse, the old hermit turns the mouse into a stout cat. When a dog threatens the stout cat, the hermit changes the cat into a big dog. When a tiger threatens the dog, the hermit changes the dog into a royal tiger, who struts around, full of pride. When the hermit reminds him of his beginnings as a mouse, the ungrateful tiger threatens to kill him. So the hermit turns him back into a mouse and again sits thinking about big and little.

© 1995 Educational Impressions, Inc.

# Questions & Activities Based Upon Bloom's Taxonomy
*Once A Mouse*

**Knowledge:**
1. What creature grabbed the mouse?
2. What was the hermit thinking about?
3. After the mouse changed into the cat, why did he hide under the hermit's bed?

**Comprehension:**
1. What special powers did the hermit have?
2. What caused the hermit to change the tiger back into a mouse?
3. The author said that the tiger "peacocked" about the forest. What did this mean?

**Application:**
1. What do you think the crow would have done to the mouse?
2. Explain the difference between a tiger and a royal tiger.
3. How could you use this story to improve yourself?

**Analysis:**
1. Marcia Brown used woodcuts to illustrate this story. Compare this art style to one used in another book you've read recently.
2. Compare the mouse and tiger. How are they alike and how are they different?
3. Why, do you think, did the hermit have feeling for the mouse?

**Synthesis:**
1. What might have happened had the hermit not changed the tiger back into the mouse?
2. Create a new ending for the story.
3. Give the tiger some different characteristics. How might these have changed the tiger?

**Evaluation:**
1. What kind of person do you think the hermit was? Explain your answer.
2. Explain what lesson might be learned from this story. How could you use this lesson to improve yourself?
3. Would you have stopped and helped the mouse? Why or why not?

© 1995 Educational Impressions, Inc.

**Find out what a hermit is. Share your findings with the class.**

# Dear Hermit,

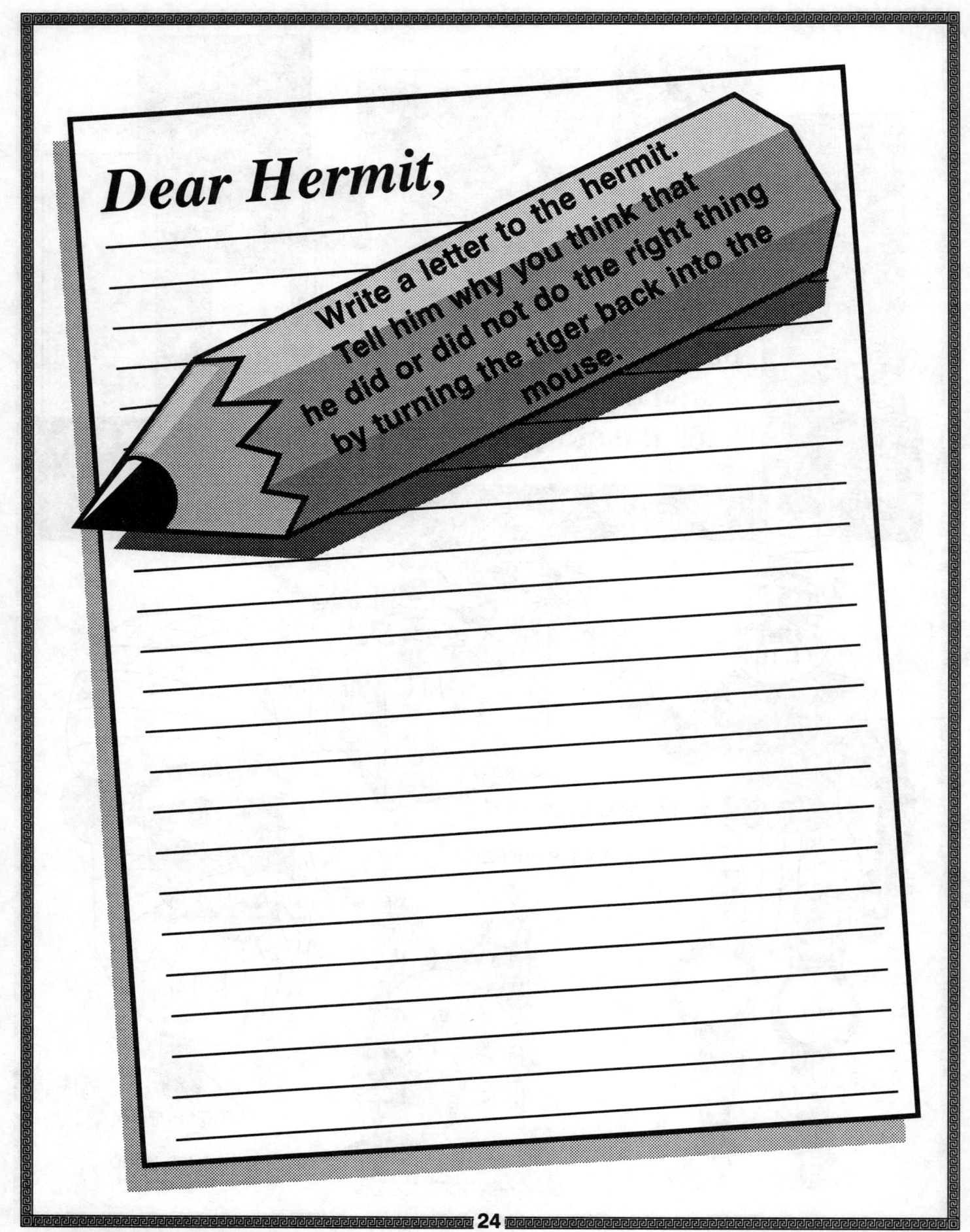

Write a letter to the hermit. Tell him why you think that he did or did not do the right thing by turning the tiger back into the mouse.

| List at least 6 things you think are big. | List at least 6 things you think are little. |
|---|---|
| _____ | _____ |
| _____ | _____ |
| _____ | _____ |
| _____ | _____ |
| _____ | _____ |
| _____ | _____ |
| _____ | _____ |
| _____ | _____ |

© 1995 Educational Impressions, Inc.

# Write a sequel
## to this story.
**What happened to the mouse after he was turned back into a mouse by the hermit?**

_____
_____
_____
_____
_____
_____
_____
_____
_____
_____
_____

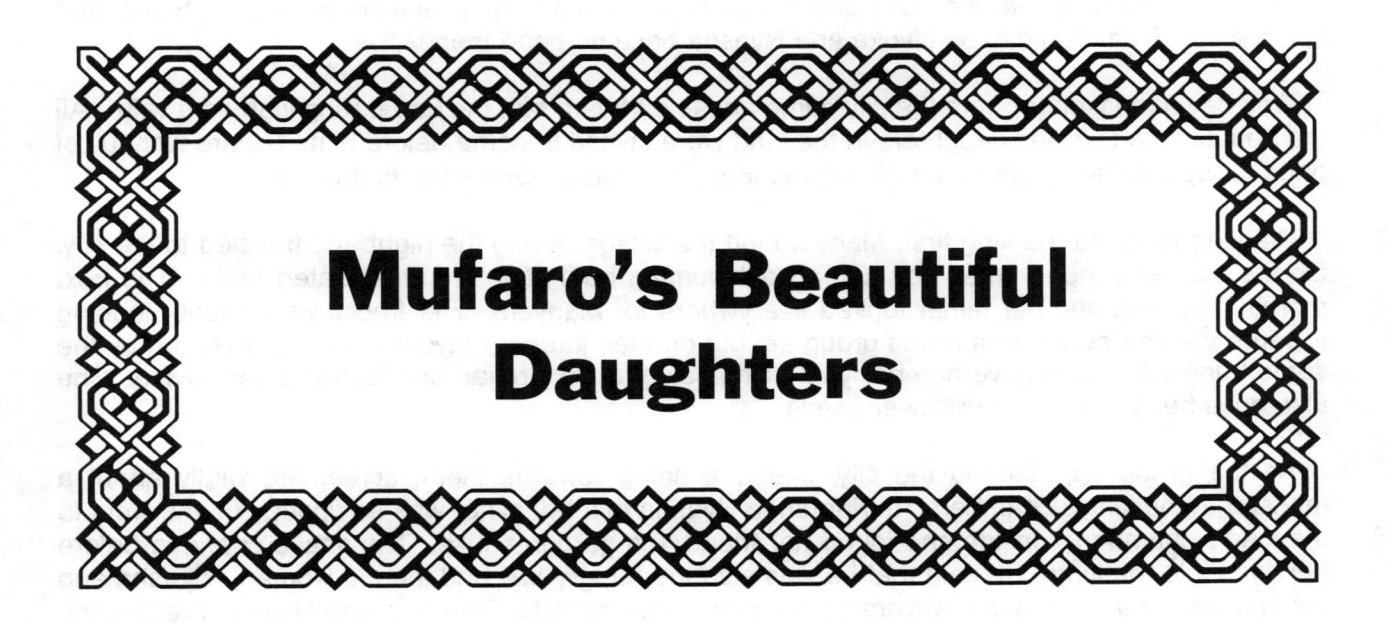

# Mufaro's Beautiful Daughters

# Mufaro's Beautiful Daughters

by John Steptoe

## STORY SUMMARY

Mufaro lived in a small village in Africa with his two beautiful daughters, Manyara and Nyasha. Manyara was always in a bad mood. Nyasha was sweet and caring.

Nyasha had a small garden. One day she found a small garden snake in her garden. She called him Nyoka. From that day on Nyoka and Nyasha became good friends.

One day a messenger from the city came and told Mufaro that the Great King wanted a wife. All the beautiful and worthy daughters in the land were invited to come before him. Mufaro was full of pride for both of his daughters and insisted that they would make a trip to the city.

Wanting to get to the king first, Manyara left the village during the night and traveled to the city. On the way, she met a small boy and an old woman, both of whom she treated badly. The next morning Nyasha and her father looked everywhere for Manyara. Her tracks were found heading towards the city, so the rest of the group set out on their journey. Nyasha was approached by the same hungry boy and gave him her yam. She saw the old woman and followed her advice. She also gave her a pouch of sunflower seeds.

As the group approached the city, Manyara came towards them, screaming wildly about a monster in the king's chambers. It frightened Nyasha that her sister was so upset, but she went to the king's chambers. Inside she found her friend, the garden snake. The snake changed before her eyes into the king. He said that he was also the hungry boy and the old woman. Nyasha and the king were married, and Manyara became Nyasha's servant. The king and Nyasha lived happily ever after.

© 1995 Educational Impressions, Inc.

# Questions & Activities Based Upon Bloom's Taxonomy
*Mufaro's Beautiful Daughters*

**Knowledge:**
1. What did Nyasha find under the yam vine?
2. How many daughters did Mufaro have?
3. Which daughter was mean?

**Comprehension:**
1. How did Nyasha feel about life?
2. Why did Manyara leave her father and sister?
3. How did Nyasha react to the strange woman?

**Application:**
1. Describe your relationship with a brother or sister.
2. How might you have reacted to the strange happenings?
3. How is your life different from Nyasha's?

**Analysis:**
1. Compare the two sisters. How are they alike? How are they different?
2. Read another African tale. How is it different from *Mufaro's Beautiful Daughters?*
3. Why didn't Mufaro know Manyara's true character?

**Synthesis:**
1. How might the story have been different had Manyara become queen?
2. Create another animal that might have turned into the king.
3. If you had been the king, how might you have tested Nyasha?

**Evaluation:**
1. What kind of rulers do you think the king and Nyasha were? Explain your answer.
2. This book is a Caldecott Honor Book. Tell what you like or don't like about the art work in this book.
3. This story teaches a lesson. What is that lesson?

© 1995 Educational Impressions, Inc.

**The snake is a reptile. List as many reptiles as you can.**

_____   _____
_____   _____
_____   _____
_____   _____
_____   _____
_____   _____

Draw a picture of a reptile you might like to have as a pet.

© 1995 Educational Impressions, Inc.

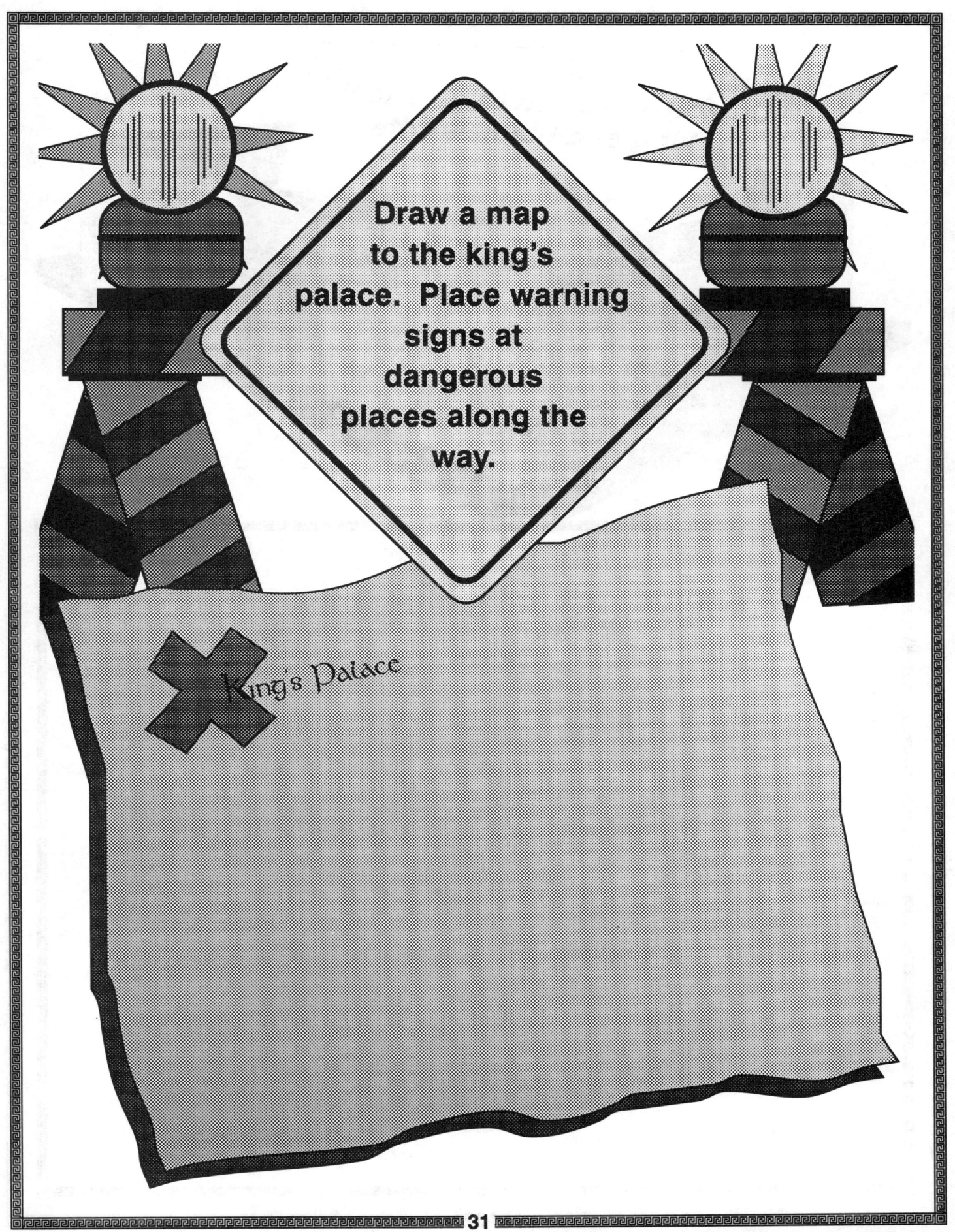

**Draw a map to the king's palace. Place warning signs at dangerous places along the way.**

King's Palace

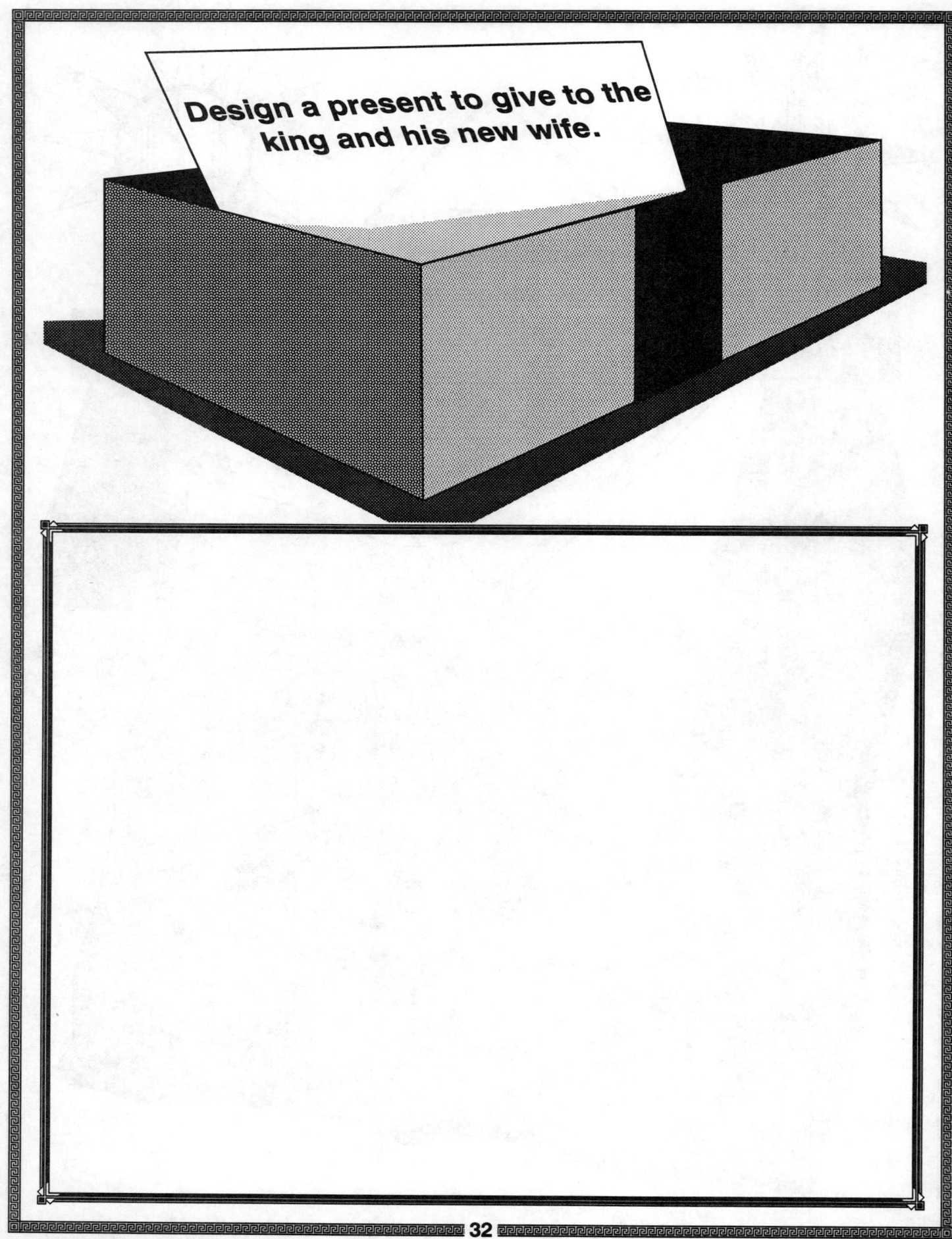

**Design a present to give to the king and his new wife.**

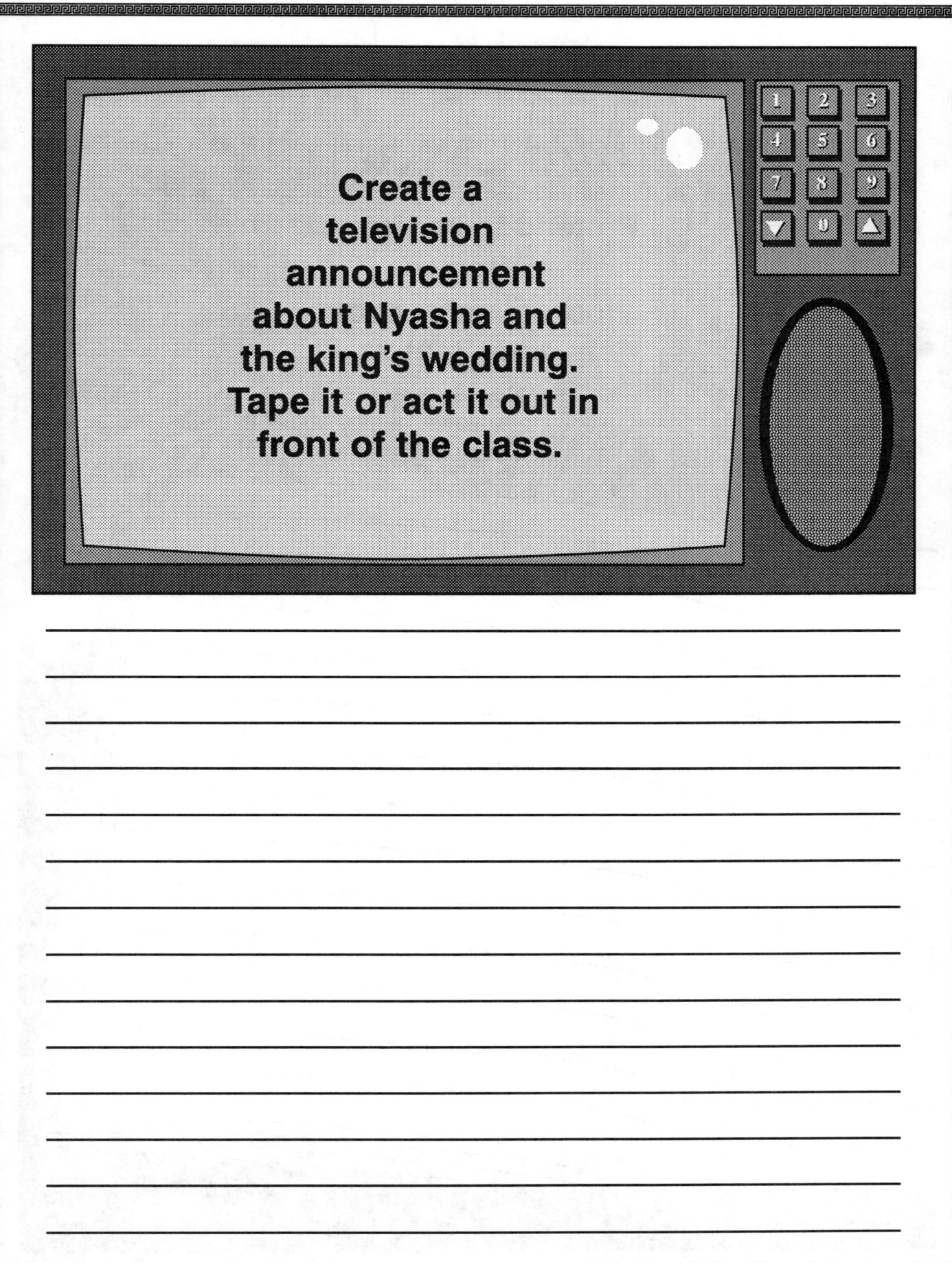

Create a television announcement about Nyasha and the king's wedding. Tape it or act it out in front of the class.

Pretend to be Nyasha. Write a journal entry about meeting with the garden snake.

**Draw a picture that shows where Nyasha and the king will live.**

# Pretend to be Manyara.

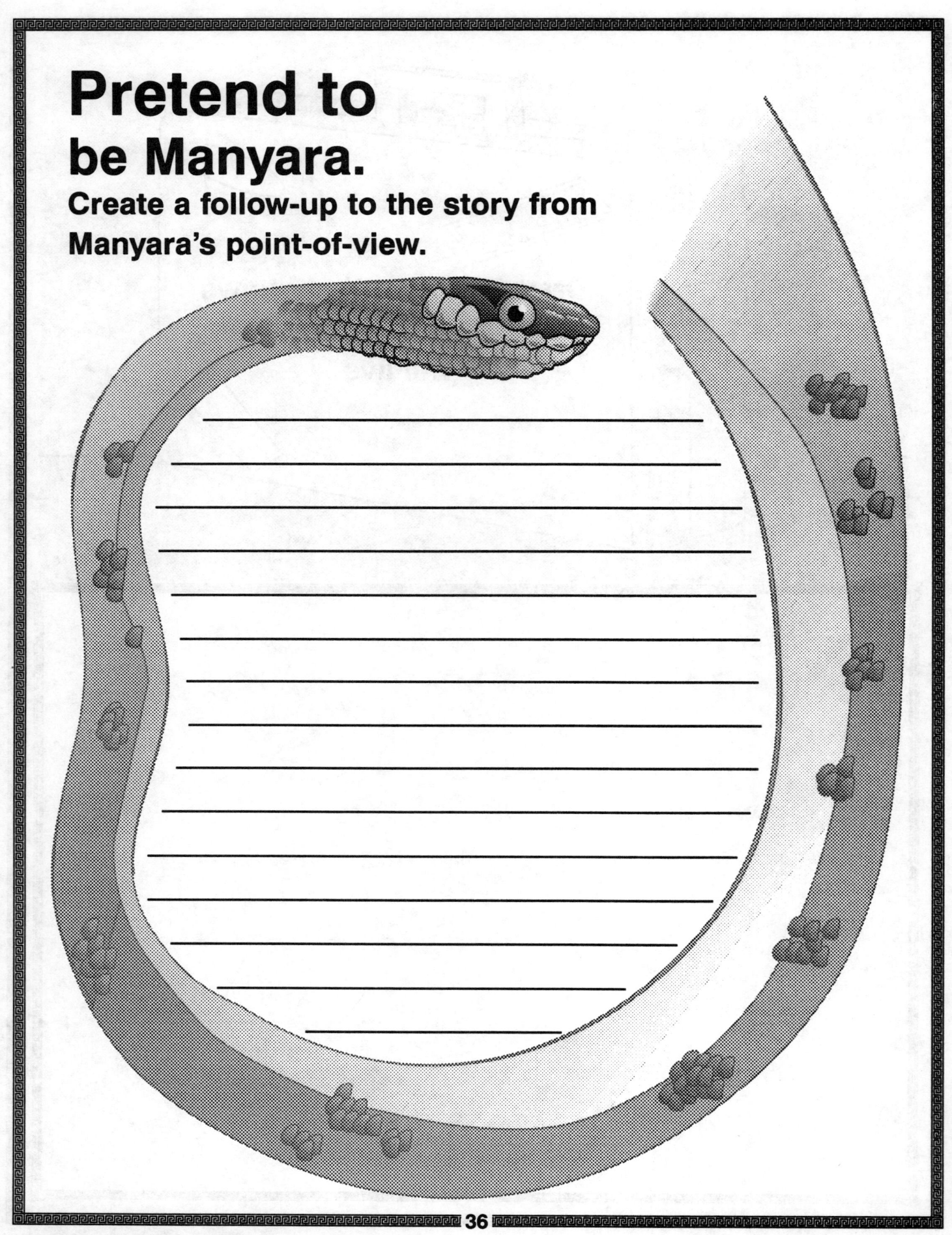

**Create a follow-up to the story from Manyara's point-of-view.**

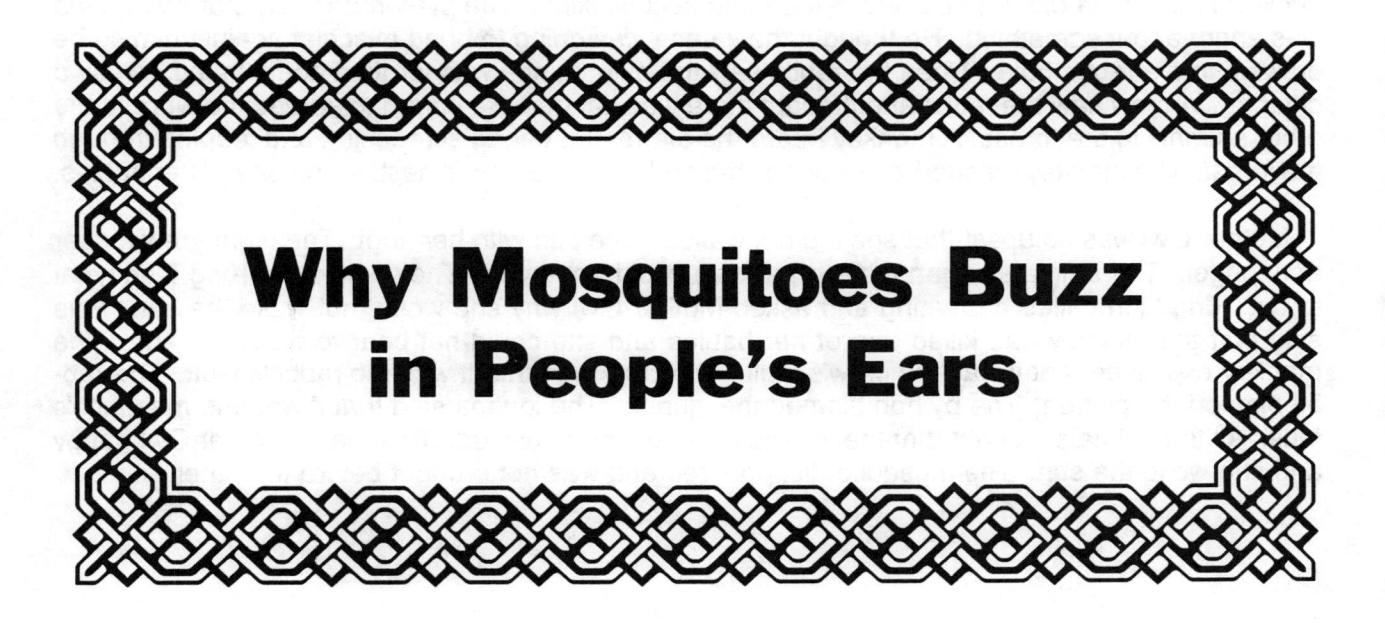

# Why Mosquitoes Buzz in People's Ears

# Why Mosquitoes Buzz in People's Ears

by Verna Aardema

## STORY SUMMARY

One day a mosquito told the iguana that he saw a farmer digging yams as big as the mosquito. The iguana was disgusted at the mosquito's tale and left, sticking two sticks into his ears so he could not hear the mosquito. As the iguana traveled through the forest, a python saw him and spoke. The iguana did not hear the python and kept walking. The python decided that the iguana was angry about something. He thought the iguana was going to bring mischief against him so he crawled into a rabbit hole. When the rabbit saw the python, she was terrified and jumped across a clearing. A crow saw the rabbit and thought there was danger. He began to spread the word to the other animals in the forest. A monkey heard the alarm and began screeching and leaping through the forest. The monkey crashed into a dead limb and fell into an owl's nest, killing one of her babies.

Mother Owl was so upset that she did not wake up the sun with her hoot. The night grew longer and longer. The animals began to fear that day would not come. They asked the King Lion what to do. King Lion called a meeting and asked Mother Owl why she would not wake the sun. She said that the monkey had killed one of her babies and she could not bear to wake the sun. The monkey explained that it was the crow's fault. The crow said that it was the rabbit's fault. The rabbit blamed the python. The python blamed the iguana. The iguana said that it was the mosquito's fault. All the animals thought that the mosquito should be punished. This made Mother Owl happy and she woke the sun. The mosquito disappeared and was not brought before the other animals.

© 1995 Educational Impressions, Inc.

# Questions & Activities Based Upon Bloom's Taxonomy
*Why Mosquitoes Buzz in People's Ears*

**Knowledge:**
1. What did the iguana stick in his ears as he left the waterhole?
2. How did the monkey kill the owlet?
3. Who was the king?

**Comprehension:**
1. Why did the crow feel it was his duty to spread an alarm?
2. Explain how the monkey tried to convince the king that he was not responsible for the owlet's death.
3. The sun would not wake up. Why?

**Application:**
1. This type of story is sometimes called a pattern book. Explain why.
2. Explain to the iguana why he should not put sticks in his ears.
3. Has anyone ever told you a tale you did not believe? If so, share it with your classmates.

**Analysis:**
1. Compare this pattern book to another pattern book that you might have read. How are they alike and how are they different?
2. Which is your favorite character and why?
3. Choose two characters in the story and compare them. Tell how they are alike and how they are different.

**Synthesis:**
1. How might the story have been different had the sun not woken up?
2. Predict how you might have handled the problem of who was to blame for the baby owl's death.
3. Add two more animals that caused problems in the story.

**Evaluation:**
1. How do you think mosquito felt about the baby owl's death? Why?
2. Was the mosquito punished correctly for his part in the story? Why or why not?
3. Do you think that this is a good title for this tale? Explain.

© 1995 Educational Impressions, Inc.

**Have a trial involving King Lion as the judge, the mosquito as the defendant, and the other animals as the jury.**

**Prepare some arguments in the mosquito's behalf.**
_____
_____
_____
_____
_____
_____
_____

**Prepare some arguments against the mosquito.**
_____
_____
_____
_____
_____
_____
_____

© 1995 Educational Impressions, Inc.

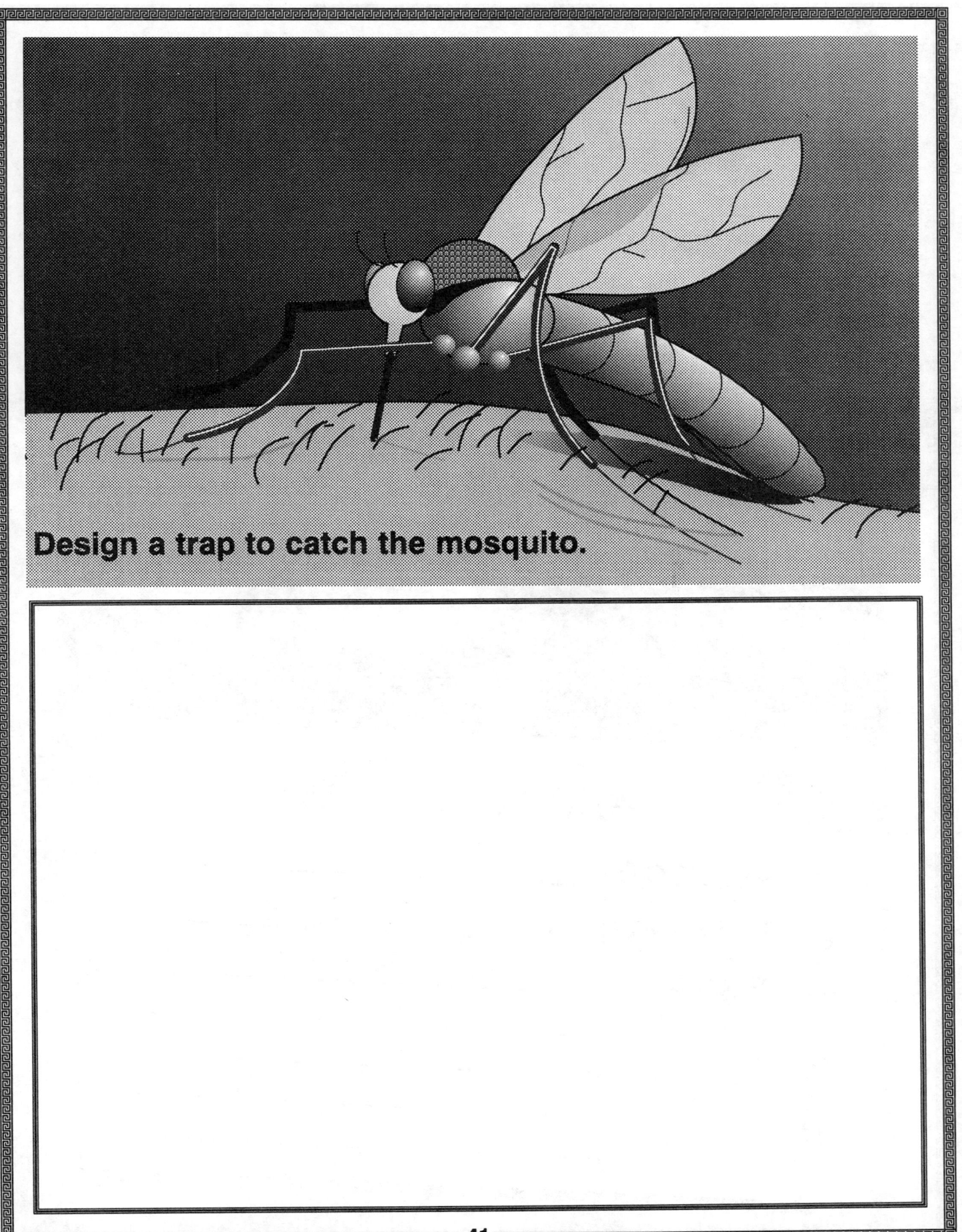

**Design a trap to catch the mosquito.**

41

Choose one of the animals in this story and find out more about it. Report your findings to your friends.

# FACT FILE

**SUBJECT:** _____

**RESOURCE:** _____

**FACTS:** _____
_____
_____
_____
_____

© 1995 Educational Impressions, Inc.

**The mosquito is an insect. List as many different insects as you can.**

_____
_____
_____
_____
_____
_____
_____

**Draw a picture of one of the insects listed above.**

© 1995 Educational Impressions, Inc.

# Choose a character
## from another legend.
**Create your own pattern book with that character in it.**

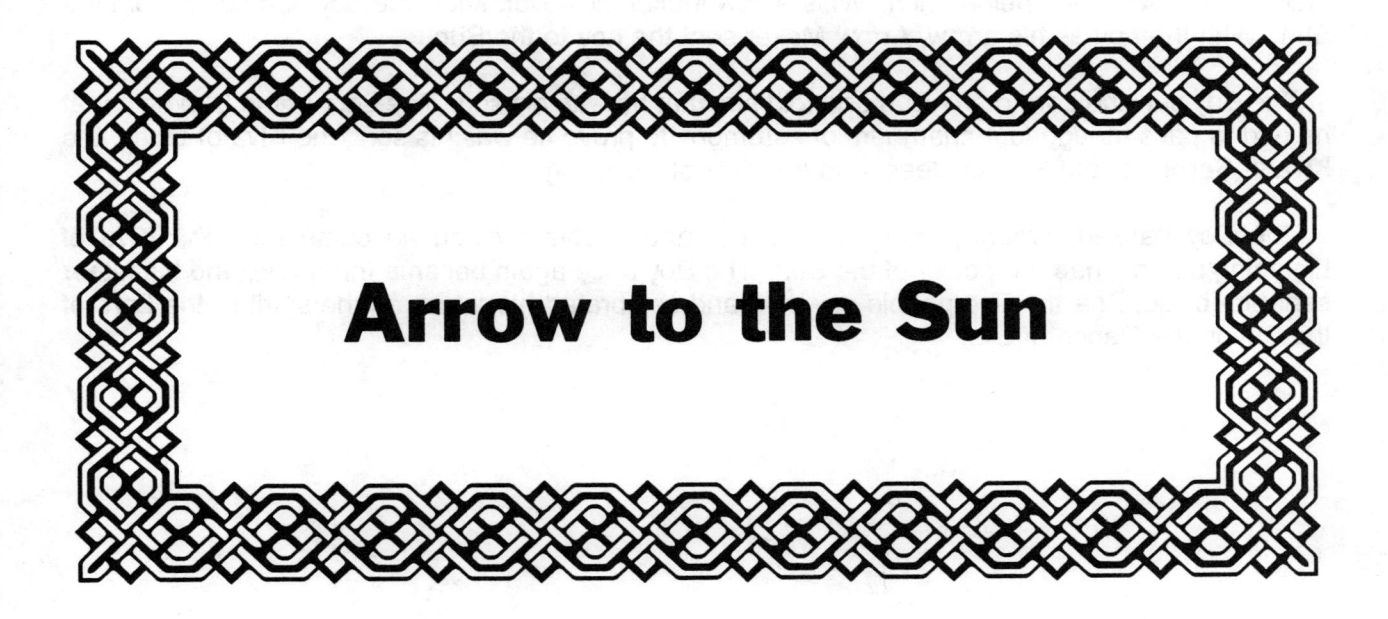

# Arrow to the Sun

# Arrow to the Sun

by Gerald McDermott

## STORY SUMMARY

Long ago the Sun sent a spark of life to the earth. A few months later a baby boy was born. The boy grew up in a pueblo, but the other children of the pueblo ostracized him because he did not have a father.

One day the boy left home to search for his father. Along the way, he met Corn Planter and Pot Maker, but neither one helped him. Wise Arrow Maker, however, knew the boy had come from the Sun. With the boy as his arrow, Arrow Maker sent the boy to the Sun.

The Boy saw the Lord of the Sun and told him that he was his son. The Lord of the Sun said that he had to pass though four chambers of ceremony to prove he was his son: the Kiva of Lions, the Kiva of Serpents, the Kiva of Bees, and the Kiva of Lightning.

The Boy passed through each Kiva without any trouble. When he came from the Kiva of Lightning he, too, had the power of the Sun. The Boy once again became the arrow, and his father sent him back to earth. The people saw him and celebrated his return as the spirit of the Lord of the Sun in the Dance of Life.

© 1995 Educational Impressions, Inc.

# Questions & Activities Based Upon Bloom's Taxonomy
*Arrow To The Sun*

**Knowledge:**
1. How did the spark of life travel to the earth?
2. What is the name for the boy's home?
3. What kind of weapons did Arrow Maker create?

**Comprehension:**
1. Why were the children mean to the boy?
2. Describe Corn Planter's job.
3. Explain how the boy got to the Sun.

**Application:**
1. Describe your version of the boy's battle with the snakes.
2. Have you ever had to complete a task that seemed impossible? Describe it.
3. How might you have handled the children making fun of you if you had been the Boy.

**Analysis:**
1. Why, do you think, were people happy to see the Boy after his journey to the Sun?
2. Describe an important characteristic the Boy has.
3. Of the four Kivas, which do you think was the hardest? Why?

**Synthesis:**
1. What might have happened to the Boy had he not passed each trial of the Kivas? How would this have changed the outcome of the story?
2. Create two other Kivas the Boy might have to conquer to prove his worthiness. Describe these Kivas.
3. Describe how the Boy might have changed his village for the better.

**Evaluation:**
1. Was it right for the children to make fun of the Boy? Why or why not?
2. Would you like to be the Boy and go on the same journey? Why or why not?
3. What lesson can be learned from this legend?

© 1995 Educational Impressions, Inc.

**The Boy was very brave. Tell about a time when you were brave.**

*I was brave when...*

**MEDAL OF BRAVERY**

**Draw a picture that illustrates that event.**

**Illustrate a picture of another Kiva the Boy might have had to conquer.**

**Using hardening clay, create a pot. Paint it with Pueblo designs similar to those in the story.**

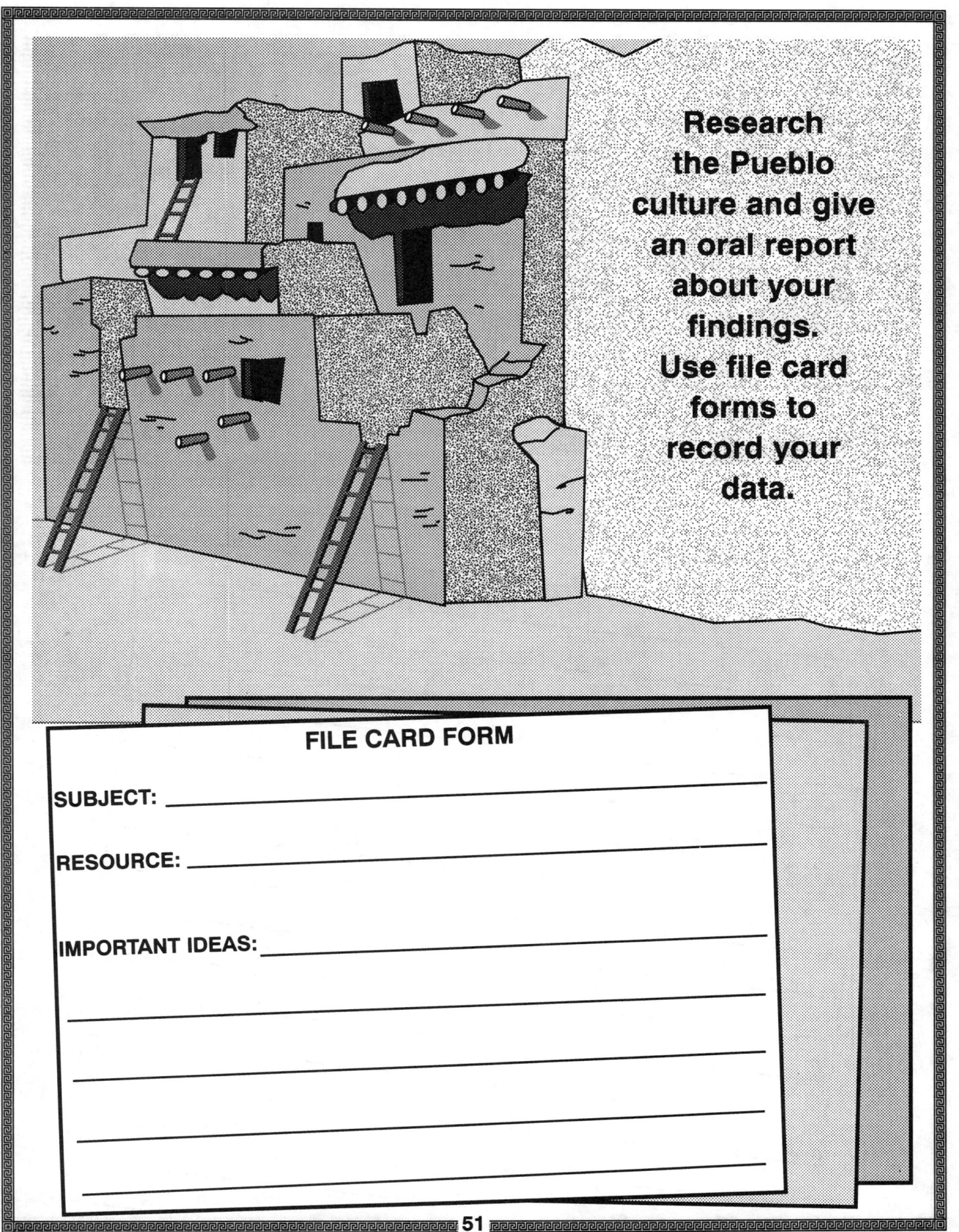

Research the Pueblo culture and give an oral report about your findings. Use file card forms to record your data.

### FILE CARD FORM

SUBJECT: _____

RESOURCE: _____

IMPORTANT IDEAS: _____
_____
_____
_____
_____
_____
_____

© 1995 Educational Impressions, Inc.

**Write a letter from the Boy to his mother thanking her for raising him the way she did.**

Dear Mother,

© 1995 Educational Impressions, Inc.

Draw a picture that shows why the sun is so important to us.

# Write a newspaper article
## about the Boy's adventure.
**Remember, a newspaper article should include only facts, not opinion.**

# The Legend of the Bluebonnet

# The Legend of the Bluebonnet

by Tomie de Paola

## STORY SUMMARY

Many years ago the Comanches were taken with drought. They danced for three days to the Great Spirits, asking for rain. Many of the tribe had died of starvation and sickness because of the drought and famine. Among the tribe was a little girl named She-Who-Is-Alone.

As the sun was setting, the shaman came out of the hills and told the tribe that the Great Spirits had spoken to him. He told the people that they must give up their most prized possessions to the Great Spirits to replace what the people had taken from Mother Earth. When this sacrifice was made, the drought and famine would cease. The Earth would be restored to the people.

Only She-Who-Is-Alone was willing to sacrifice her most prized possession. Her parents and grandparents had died from the famine. That night She-Who-Is-Alone waited until everyone was asleep. She walked out into the hills with her beloved warrior doll, which had a beautiful blue feather in its headdress. She told the Great Spirits that the doll was the only thing she had left from her dead family. The doll was her most prized possession. She asked the Great Spirits to accept it as her sacrifice.

She-Who-Is-Alone gathered twigs and leaves, then started a fire. She placed the warrior doll in the fire and burned it. She gathered up the ashes and cast them into the wind. The girl then fell asleep. When she awoke, the hills were covered with beautiful blue flowers, as blue as the feather in the doll's headdress.

When the people saw the miraculous sight, they danced with joy. Rain began to fall and the land became alive again. From that day on, She-Who-Is-Alone was known as One-Who-Dearly-Loved-Her-People. Every spring the Great Spirits remember the little girl's sacrifice and cover the hills with beautiful blue flowers.

© 1995 Educational Impressions, Inc.

# Questions & Activities Based Upon Bloom's Taxonomy
*The Legend of the Bluebonnet*

**Knowledge:**
1. Why were the people singing?
2. How many days did the dancers dance?
3. What Indian tribe is this legend about?

**Comprehension:**
1. Describe the drought.
2. Why was She-Who-Is-Alone's doll so special to her?
3. Describe the people's attitude during this time in their lives.

**Application:**
1. As She-Who-Is-Alone, describe your life after losing your parents.
2. What would you have given up had you been asked to make a sacrifice?
3. Who is the shaman? Why is he so special?

**Analysis:**
1. Compare She-Who-Is-Alone to other people in her tribe. How are they alike? How are they different?
2. How do you think the people abused the earth, bringing on the famine?
3. List the good qualities She-Who-Is-Alone possesses.

**Synthesis:**
1. Suppose the girl had not given up her doll. How might the story have been different?
2. Predict how the girl's sacrifice changed the tribe.
3. Imagine you were one of the Indian children in the story. How would you have felt toward She-Who-Is-Alone after the great sacrifice she made for her tribe. Explain your feelings.

**Evaluation:**
1. Would you have been brave enough to give up your doll had you been the girl? Why or why not?
2. The Comanches moved around many times during the seasons. Would you have liked to have been a Comanche during those times? Why or why not?
3. How can we apply this story to our own lives and our world?

© 1995 Educational Impressions, Inc.

# R.I.P.

**Make-up an elegy to She-Who-Is-Alone's doll. Illustrate it.**

**An elegy is a song or poem expressing grief about someone's death. Write your elergy here.**

_____
_____
_____
_____
_____
_____
_____
_____

© 1995 Educational Impressions, Inc.

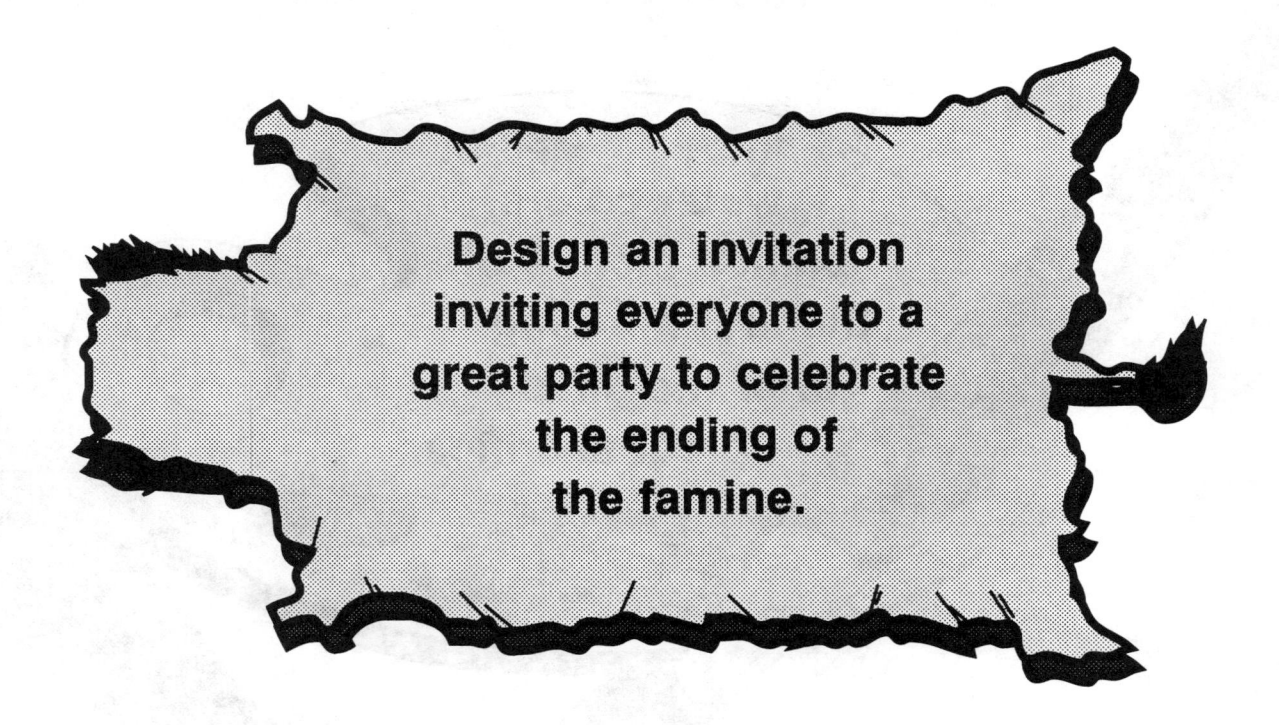

Design an invitation inviting everyone to a great party to celebrate the ending of the famine.

**Using water colors, paint a picture of the first morning after the girl's great sacrifice.**

Sketch your idea here.

© 1995 Educational Impressions, Inc.

**Research the Comanche culture. Write at least five things that you learn.**

1. _____
_____
2. _____
_____
3. _____
_____
4. _____
_____
5. _____
_____

© 1995 Educational Impressions, Inc.

# Write an original legend
about how your
state flower came to be.

# Strega Nona

# Strega Nona

retold by Tomie de Paola

## STORY SUMMARY

In a town, long ago, lived an old woman named Strega Nona, which meant "Grandma Witch." Strega Nona needed help, so she hired Big Anthony to sweep the house, wash the dishes, weed the garden, pick the vegetables, feed and milk the goat, and fetch water. She would pay him three coins and give him a place to sleep and food to eat. The only thing she told him NOT to do was touch her magic pasta pot.

One evening Big Anthony heard Strega Nona singing in the kitchen to her magic pot. The pasta pot boiled and suddenly filled with steaming hot pasta. Then Strega Nona sang another song, causing the pot to stop making pasta. Big Anthony saw this and thought it was wonderful. What he didn't see was that Strega Nona blew three kisses at the pot.

Big Anthony waited for a chance to get at the pot. As soon as Strega Nona left the house, Big Anthony went to the pasta pot and sang the magic words. The pot began to boil and was soon full of hot pasta. Big Anthony called everyone from the village to bring their bowls and forks to Strega Nona's for hot pasta. The people laughed at him, but brought their bowls and forks anyway.

When everyone in town had been fed, Big Anthony sang the magic song to stop the pasta pot from boiling, but it just kept making more and more pasta. Soon the pasta was pouring out into the streets. People were running everywhere trying to escape the pasta. Big Anthony sang the magic song over and over, but the pasta kept flowing.

At last Strega Nona came up the road to town. She saw what had happened and ran to her house. She recited the magic words and blew three kisses at the pot, and the pasta stopped flowing from the pot. Everyone thanked Strega Nona for saving the town.

As for Big Anthony's punishment, he had to eat all the pasta so Strega Nona could get to her bed for a good night's sleep.

© 1995 Educational Impressions, Inc.

# Questions & Activities Based Upon Bloom's Taxonomy

*Strega Nona*

**Knowledge:**
1. What did Strega Nona use to cure headaches?
2. What is the meaning of Strega Nona?
3. Where was Strega Nona when Big Anthony sang to the magic pot?

**Comprehension:**
1. Why did the townspeople come to visit Strega Nona?
2. Describe some of Big Anthony's chores.
3. Why didn't the pot respond to Big Anthony's song asking it to stop boiling?

**Application:**
1. Why did the people laugh at Big Anthony?
2. What would you do if you saw pasta flowing down the streets in your town?
3. How might you have punished Big Anthony?

**Analysis:**
1. Compare this story to another that uses a magic pot or magic utensil (one example is *The Funny Little Woman*). How are these two stories alike and how are they different?
2. What three questions might you ask Big Anthony about his experience with the magic pot?
3. Often the word "witch" means something evil or scary. What characteristics do you think of when describing Strega Nona?

**Synthesis:**
1. Suppose Strega Nona had not returned until much later. What might she have found when she returned?
2. Guess where Strega Nona got the magic pot. Give a little background about the pot's previous owner.
3. How might Strega Nona have prevented Big Anthony from causing the magic pot to make pasta?

**Evaluation:**
1. Was Big Anthony's punishment fitting? Why or why not?
2. Do you think Big Anthony ever touched the magic pot again? Why or why not?
3. Would you like a magic pot? What would you do with it?

© 1995 Educational Impressions, Inc.

Create a way to stop the pasta from running over the village.

66

© 1995 Educational Impressions, Inc.

Discover what pasta is made from and how it is made. Find some pictures or draw some to show the process. Share your findings with the class.

**Write two new verses of the magic song to start and stop the magic pot.**

_____
_____
_____
_____
_____
_____
_____
_____
_____
_____
_____
_____
_____

© 1995 Educational Impressions, Inc.

**PASTA 4 SALE**

Design a way to package and sell the pasta.

Create a menu with pasta as one of the courses.

**Menu:**

**Design a mobile of your favorite foods.**

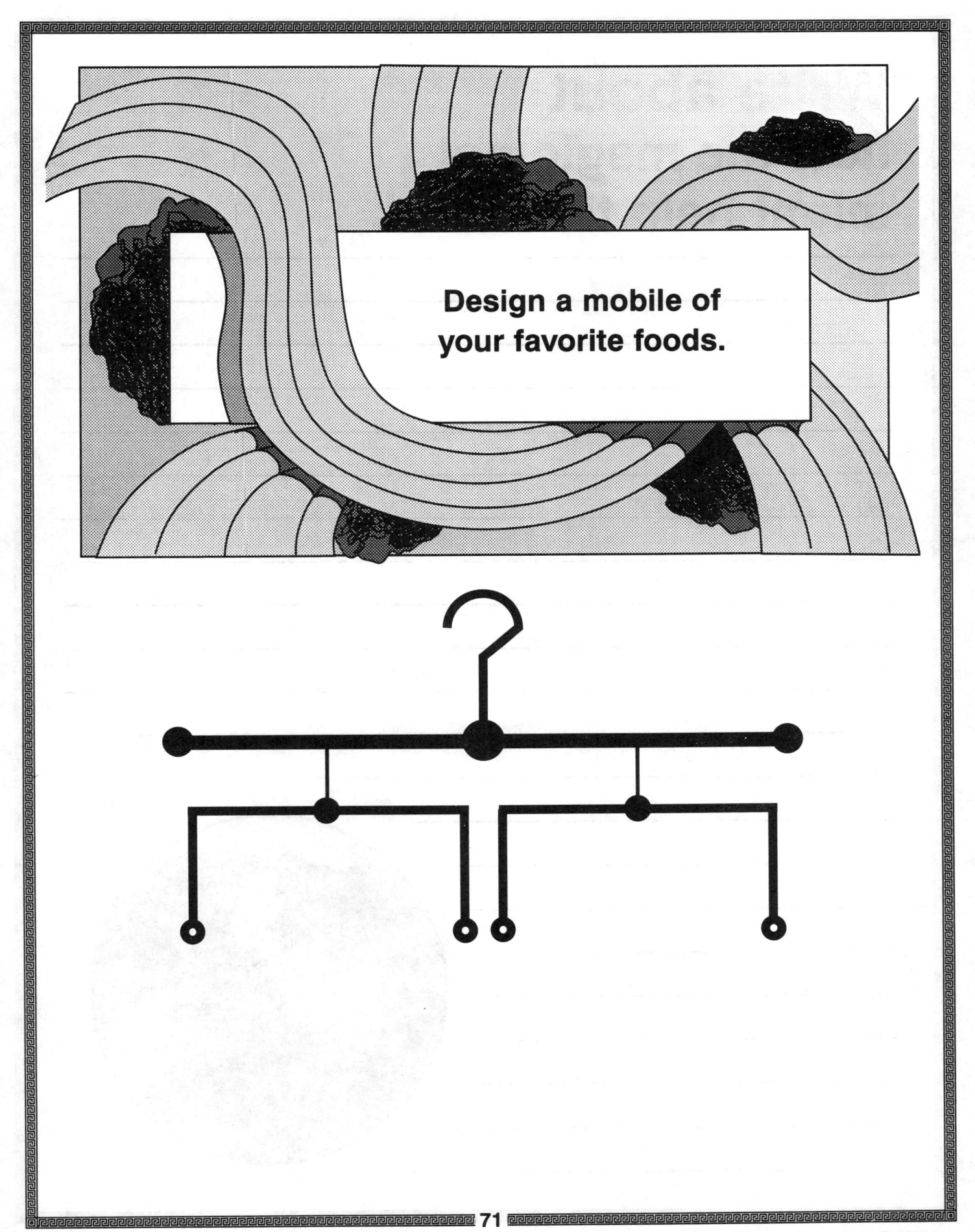

# Write about
## how the magic pot might help the world.

# The Girl Who Loved Wild Horses

# The Girl Who Loved Wild Horses

by Paul Golbe

## STORY SUMMARY

In the village lived a girl who loved horses. Each day after helping her mother, she went to the horses and stayed with them. One day she fell asleep in the meadow beside the horses. A faint rumble of thunder could be heard in the distance. The peaceful afternoon turned into an angry thunderstorm. This scared the horses, and they began to run. The girl woke up, grabbed a horse's mane, and jumped onto its back. The horses ran for a long time to escape the storm.

When the horses finally stopped, they were far from their village. The horses and the girl settled down to sleep. When they awoke, a beautiful spotted stallion, who was the leader of all the wild horses, welcomed the herd to live with him. The people searched for the girl and horses, but could not find them. A year later two hunters found the girl and brought her back to the village.

The girl was glad to see her parents, but she missed her wild horses and became ill. Her parents loved her a great deal and wanted her to be well. They gave her a beautiful dress and the best horse to ride. The stallion led the horses down the hills and waited for the girl. The wild horses were given colorful blankets to wear. Designs were painted on their backs. The girl rode away with the wild horses.

For many years the girl rode down to the village once a year and brought her parents a colt. One year, however, she did not return and was never seen again. When the hunters saw the spotted stallion, they saw that next to him galloped a beautiful mare with a floating mane and tail. They said the girl had finally become one of the wild horses.

© 1995 Educational Impressions, Inc.

# Questions & Activities Based Upon Bloom's Taxonomy
*The Girl Who Loved Wild Horses*

**Knowledge:**
1. What was the girl's favorite animal?
2. What did the tribe hunt?
3. What is a stallion? What is a mare?

**Comprehension:**
1. Describe the girl's job with the horses.
2. Explain how the hunters caught the girl.
3. Why did the horses run away?

**Application:**
1. The girl was frightened by the storm. Describe how you feel during a thunderstorm.
2. What will the girl have to give up to live with the horses?
3. If you could live anywhere, where would you choose?

**Analysis:**
1. Compare the girl's parents to the spotted stallion. How are they alike and how are they different?
2. Why do the Indians in this story consider the horses their relatives?
3. Describe the girl's relationship with the wild horses. How was she able to communicate with the horses?

**Synthesis:**
1. Suppose the girl had not traveled with the wild horses. How might her life have been different?
2. Plan a way that the horses could be used by the Indians yet still retain their freedom.
3. Imagine you are the girl. Describe your feelings as you are running with the wild horses.

**Evaluation:**
1. Would you like to live with wild horses? Why or why not?
2. How do you think the girl's family felt when she left them to run with the wild horses? Explain your answer. How would your family feel if you left?
3. What justification did the girl have for wanting to live with the wild horses rather than with her family?

© 1995 Educational Impressions, Inc.

**Design a stencil with a pattern to be used for art projects.**

**Pretend to be the Indian girl. Convince your parents why they should let you go live with the horses. What will you say?**

Design a blanket the girl might have given her parents.

**Draw a picture of your favorite animal.**

# Create a story
## with the girl in today's world living with wild horses.

# The Talking Eggs

# The Talking Eggs

by Robert D. San Souci

## STORY SUMMARY

Many years ago there lived a poor widow with two daughters, Rose and Blanche. The older sister, Rose, was mean. She always picked on Blanche, who was sweet, kind, and very smart. The old widow liked Rose the best and made Blanche do all the work. One day, after being scolded, Blanche ran into the woods and cried. A little old woman to whom Blanche had shown kindness earlier saw her and invited her to her home.

When they arrived at the old woman's shack, Blanche saw some very unusual sights, but did not laugh at any of them, for she had promised not to laugh. Among the things she saw were a two-headed cow and strange chickens of every color. She also saw the woman remove her head to braid her hair!

The woman gave Blanche a bone that turned into rich stew and a grain of rice that grew into a potful. After they ate, the old woman sent Blanche to the chicken house to gather eggs to take home with her. Although tempted, Blanche left the gold and silver eggs that said "Don't take me." The woman had instructed her to take only those eggs that said "Take me." As Blanche neared her house she tossed the eggs over her shoulder as the old woman had told her to do. Jewels and other wonderful things appeared.

When her mother and sister saw Blanche's riches, they plotted to have Rose get riches from the woman too. Rose met the woman as planned, but unlike Blanche, she did not follow any of the woman's instructions. When sent to the chicken house for eggs, Rose saw the gold and silver eggs. She disobeyed the woman and took them.

As soon as she was away from the house, Rose threw the eggs over her shoulder. Instead of riches, however, frightening things emerged. Rose and her mother ran into the woods to escape them. They searched for the old woman and the talking eggs, but they never found them.

Blanche took her riches and went to the city to live like a grand lady.

This story was adopted from a Creole folk tale.

© 1995 Educational Impressions, Inc.

# Questions & Activities Based Upon Bloom's Taxonomy
*The Talking Eggs*

**Knowledge:**
1. Who was the mother's favorite daughter?
2. What were some things the widow and her daughters grew?
3. Where did Blanche meet the old woman?

**Comprehension:**
1. Describe some of the sights that Blanche saw as she approached the old woman's house.
2. Which eggs could Blanche take?
3. Why did Rose choose the wrong eggs?

**Application:**
1. How might you have reacted to seeing a two-headed cow?
2. What would you have done with the riches that came from the eggs?
3. What lesson can be learned from this story?

**Analysis:**
1. Give some characteristics of each sister. Categorize those characteristics into good and bad.
2. Who or what do you think the old woman really was?
3. Guess why the old woman told the girls to wait until they neared their homes before throwing the eggs over their shoulders.

**Synthesis:**
1. What other things might have come out of the eggs and chased Rose?
2. Suppose Blanche had picked up the wrong eggs. How might the story have been different?
3. Predict how Blanche's life changed after she moved to the city.

**Evaluation:**
1. Who was your favorite character? Why?
2. Did the mother and Rose get what they deserved? Why or why not?
3. Blanche moved to the city. Do you think she should have sent for her mother and sister?

© 1995 Educational Impressions, Inc.

**Draw a picture of how Blanche's city house might look.**

84
© 1995 Educational Impressions, Inc.

Create a "warning sign" that could be posted at the entrance of the woods, warning people to stay away from the old woman's shack.

**Research how to milk a cow.
Demonstrate this to your class using
a rubber glove filled with water.**

How To Milk A Cow: _____

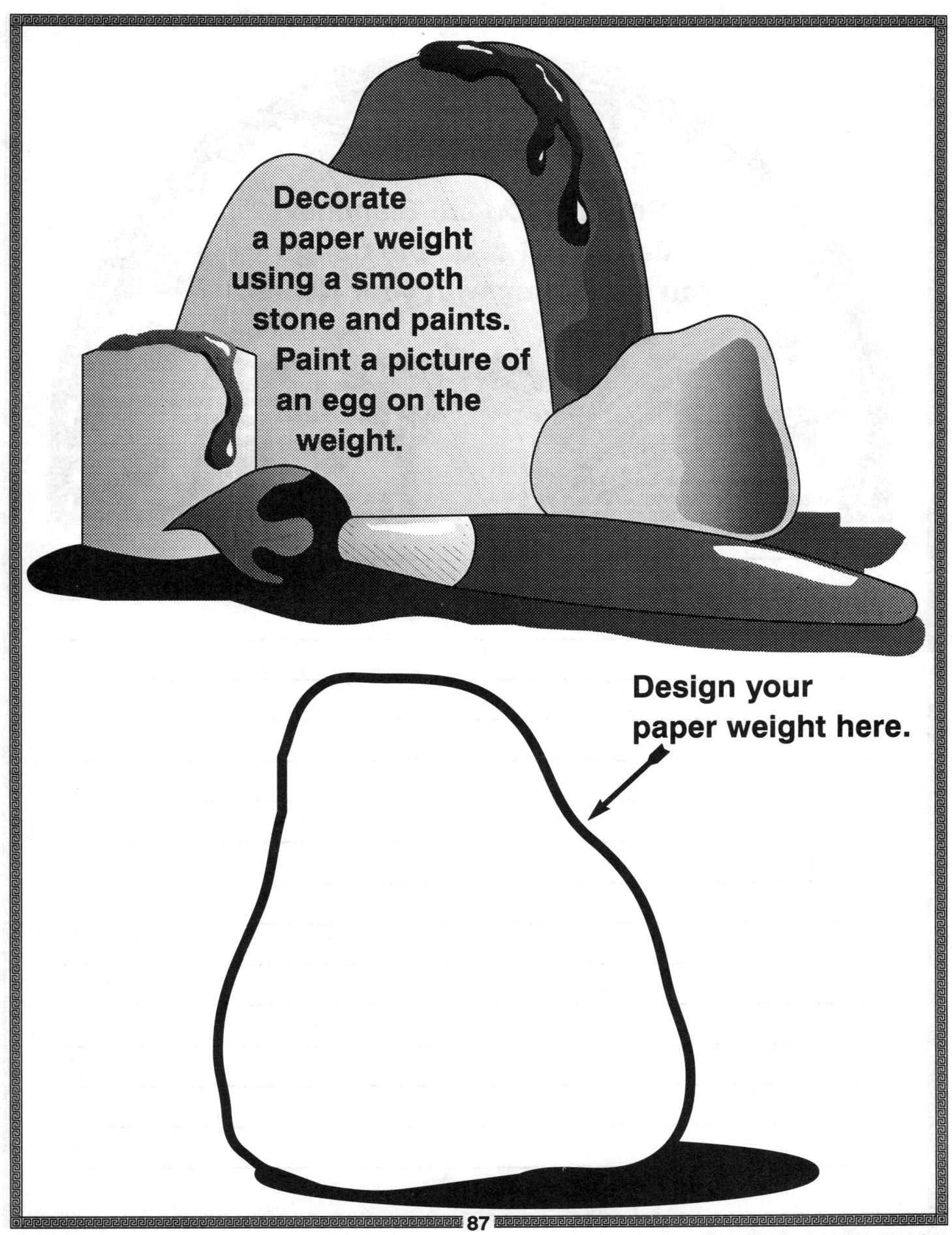

**Decorate a paper weight using a smooth stone and paints. Paint a picture of an egg on the weight.**

**Design your paper weight here.**

**Pretend you are Blanche.
Make a list of all the things
you would buy with your riches.**

# Pretend to be Blanche.
## Write a letter to the old woman thanking her for changing your life.

# Extra Activities

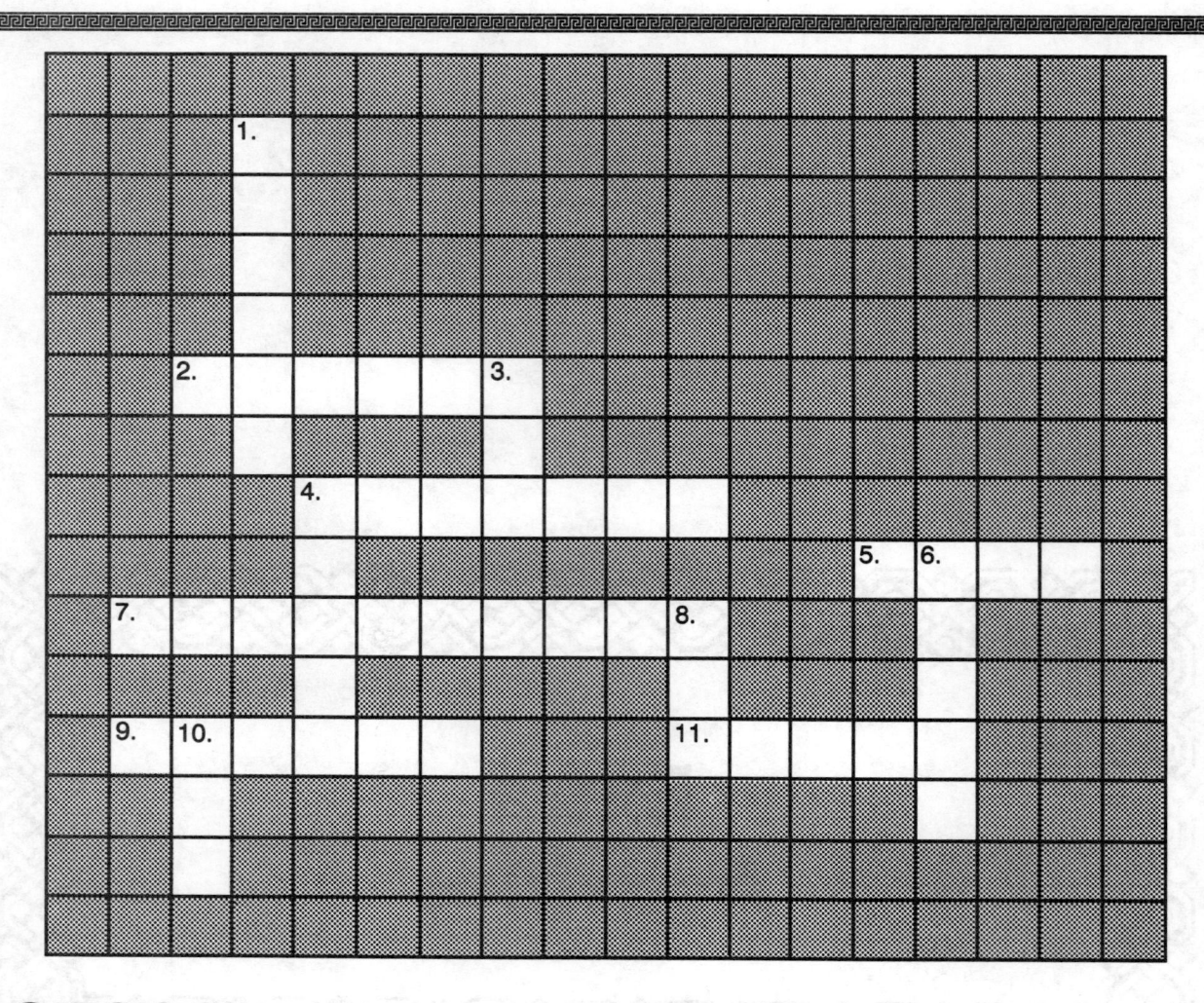

## ACROSS:

2. Blanche's eggs contained _ _ _ _ _ _ and other wonderful things.
4. The wild stallion was given a _ _ _ _ _ _ _ to wear.
5. The white globe in the sky is the _ _ _ _.
7. _ _ _ _ _ _ _ _ _ _ worked for Stega Nona.
9. Anansi was a _ _ _ _ _ _ _.
11. The tiger was once a _ _ _ _ _.

## DOWN:

1. A bluebonnet is a _ _ _ _ _ _ _.
3. The Boy traveled to the _ _ _ as an arrow.
4. The old woman took her head off to _ _ _ _ _ her hair.
6. The monkey accidentally killed an _ _ _ _ _.
8. Nyasha gave the hungry boy a _ _ _.
10. The magic _ _ _ made pasta.

# Word Scramble

1. uebloP  \_ \_ \_ \_ \_ \_

2. wrora  \_ \_ \_ \_ \_

3. gkni  \_ \_ \_ \_

4. rtgie  \_ \_ \_ \_ \_

5. nksea  \_ \_ \_ \_ \_

6. trimeh  \_ \_ \_ \_ \_ \_

7. gesg  \_ \_ \_ \_

8. qtmsoiou  \_ \_ \_ \_ \_ \_ \_ \_

9. fuaolbf  \_ \_ \_ \_ \_ \_ \_

10. ynomke  \_ \_ \_ \_ \_ \_

11. apsat  \_ \_ \_ \_ \_

12. elnchaB  \_ \_ \_ \_ \_ \_ \_

13. netobnlbeu  \_ \_ \_ \_ \_ \_ \_ \_ \_ \_

14. drepis  \_ \_ \_ \_ \_ \_

15. suoem  \_ \_ \_ \_ \_

# ANSWERS

## WORD SCRAMBLE

1. Pueblo
2. arrow
3. king
4. tiger
5. snake
6. hermit
7. eggs
8. mosquito
9. buffalo
10. monkey
11. pasta
12. Blanche
13. bluebonnet
14. spider
15. mouse

## CROSSWORD PUZZLE

**ACROSS**
2. jewels
4. blanket
5. moon
7. Big Anthony
9. spider
11. mouse

**DOWN**
1. flower
3. sun
4. braid
6. owlet
8. yam
10. pot

© 1995 Educational Impressions, Inc.

# Pencil Toppers

95

© 1995 Educational Impressions, Inc.

# Bibliography

Aardema, Verna. *Why Mosquitoes Buzz in People's Ears*. New York: The Dial Press, 1975.

Brown, Marcia. *Once A Mouse*. New York: Charles Scribner's Sons, 1961.

de Paola, Tomie. *The Legend of the Bluebonnet*. New York: Putnum Publishing Group, 1983.

_____. *Strega Nona*. New Jersey: Prentice Hall, Inc., 1975.

Golbe, Paul. *The Girl Who Loved Horses*. New York: Macmillan Publishing Company, 1978.

McDermott, Gerald. *Anansi the Spider : a tale from the Ashanti*. New York: Holt, Rienhart and Winston, 1972.

McDermott, Gerald. *Arrow to the Sun*. New York: Viking Press, 1974.

San Succi, Robert. D. *The Talking Eggs*. New York: Dial Books for Young Readers, 1989.

Steptoe, John. *Mufaro's Beautiful Daughters*. New York: Lothrop, Lee, & Shepard Books, 1987.

© 1995 Educational Impressions, Inc.